INCREDIBLE ARTHROPODS

Insects, spiders & more!

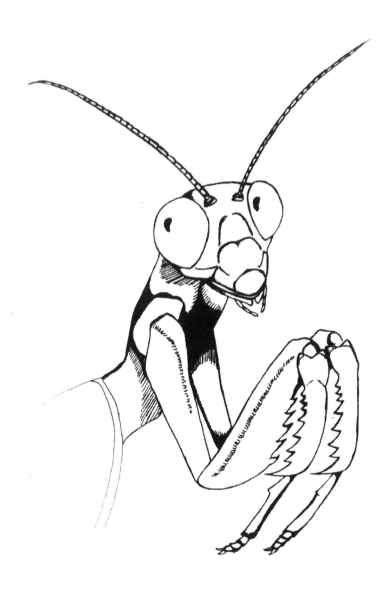

Written and Illustrated by

Kristie Reddick & Jessica Honaker

We've always wanted rainbow hair. You can make that happen.

Copyright

About the Authors:

Kristie Reddick and Jessica Honaker are entomologists who love to teach about insects and other arthropods. After receiving their Masters degrees in entomology from Texas A&M University, they created The Bug Chicks, an online entomological adventure featuring a web series and popular blog. They blend science, art, journalism and video production to inspire people young and old to learn about arthropods. For more information, free videos and podcasts visit: www.thebugchicks.com.

International Standard Book Number
ISBN 978-1-62209-502-5

This coloring book...

...contains images of insects, spiders and other **arthropods**! When we travel, we film and photograph many different species and the drawings in this book are based on real animals we have seen. This book is designed to grow with you. Your parents can read it to you at first. As you get older, you can read the information and descriptions yourself. In the back of this book, there is a glossary of terms, so if you see a word in **bold print**, check the last page to learn what it means!

We hope you enjoy it!

Sincerely,

Kristie and Jessica
The Bug Chicks

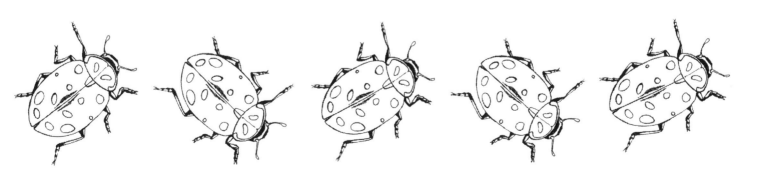

Short-horned Grasshopper

Grasshoppers are easy to identify by their long, **saltatorial** hind legs. These insects are herbivorous and use their powerful mandibles to chew up plant material. They have taste receptors on their **tarsal pads.** This means that grasshoppers can taste a leaf they are sitting on with their feet!

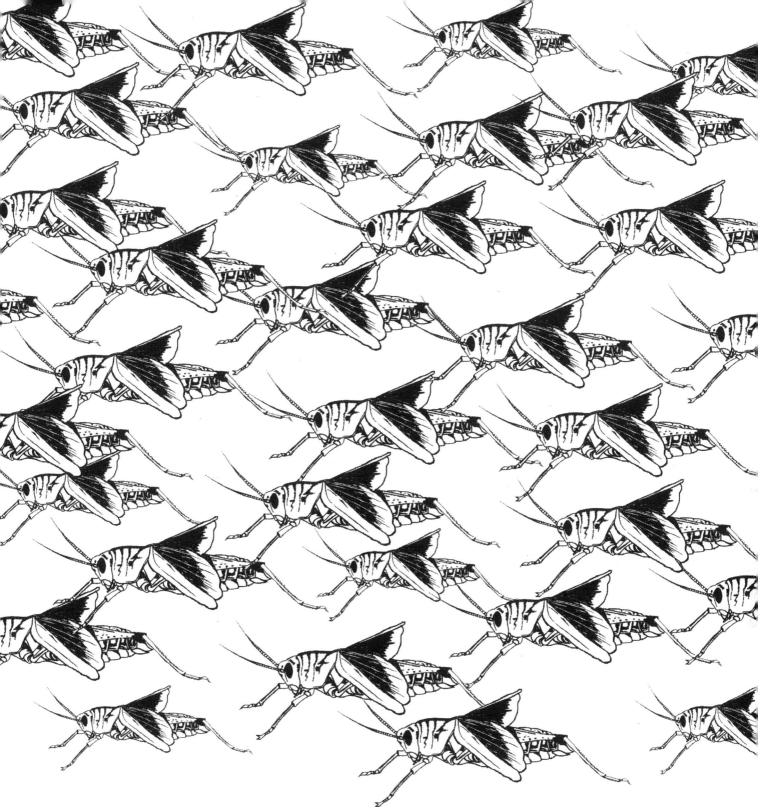

Locust Swarm

Certain short-horned grasshoppers are called locusts, because they behave differently from others. They have two different phases: solitary and **gregarious**. In the solitary phase they are harmless, feeding alone like normal grasshoppers. In the gregarious phase (which is triggered by a chemical cue) the grasshoppers grow long wings, get more colorful and start to behave as a giant mass. Young locusts hop over the ground in bands and eat everything in their path. Adult locusts fly and can number in the millions, destroying crops as they go.

Hercules Beetle

Male hercules beetles have two long horns. The lower horn extends from the head and the top horn is an extension of the **pronotum** on the thorax. They use these horns to wrestle other males for mating rights. Females do not have horns! When males and females of the same species look different it is called **dimorphism.** Hercules beetles are the largest beetles in the United States!

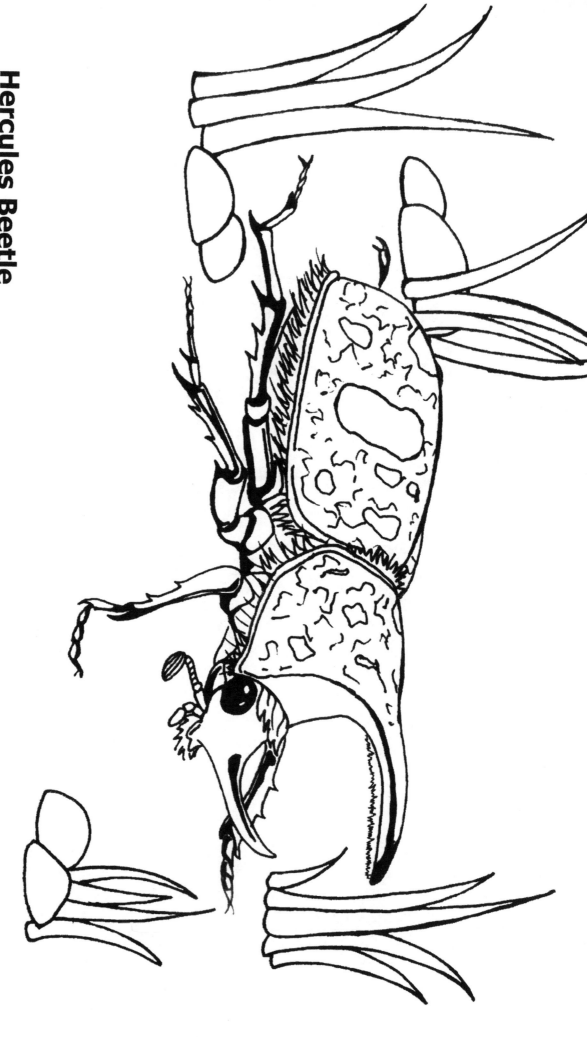

Atlas Moth

This is one of the largest moth species in the world! They are found in southeast Asia. Adult atlas moths do not have functioning mouthparts and therefore do not eat. Look closely at the tips of the forewings. They are patterned in a way that makes them look like snake heads. This form of **mimicry** serves to protect the moth from potential predators.

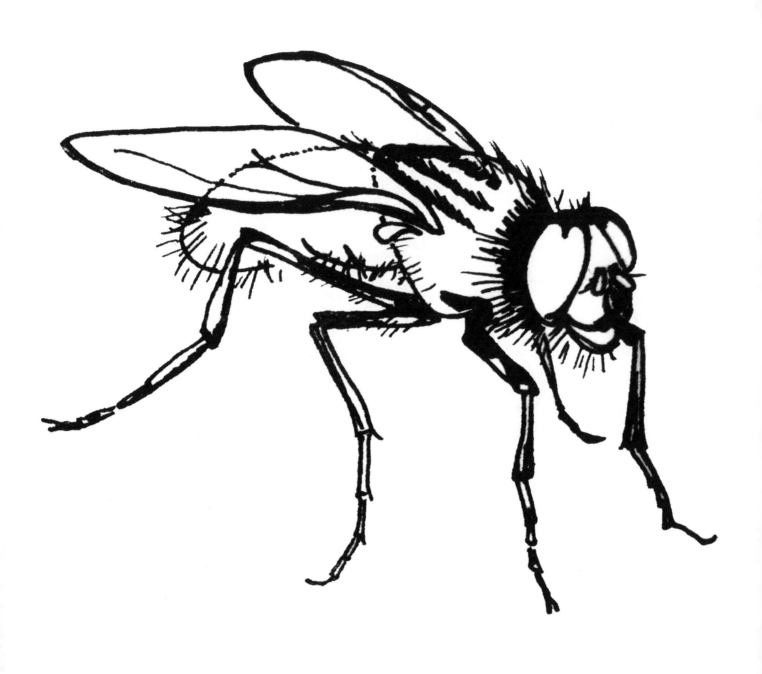

House Flies

House flies are true flies and have only one pair of wings. It doesn't slow them down- these insects are incredible fliers. The hind wings on true flies are modified into small flight stabilizers called halteres that allow them to perform aerial acrobatics. A house fly is easy to identify. Just look for four black stripes on the thorax.

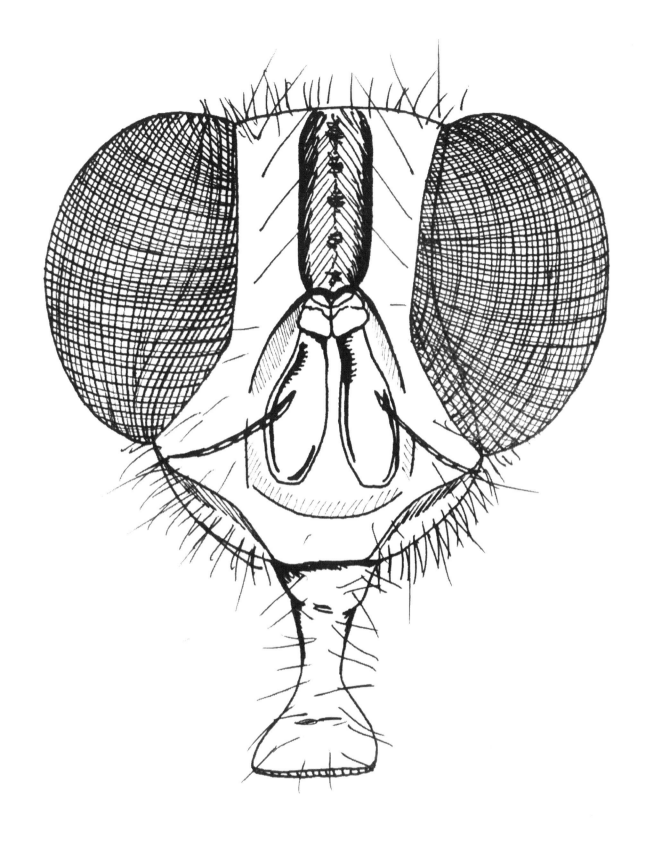

House Fly (face)

This is an **anterior** view of a house fly. You can clearly see its large eyes. Each compound eye is made up of thousands of tiny lenses called ocelli. See that cool mouthpart? It is the **labellum** and it sops up liquid food like big, spongy tongue.

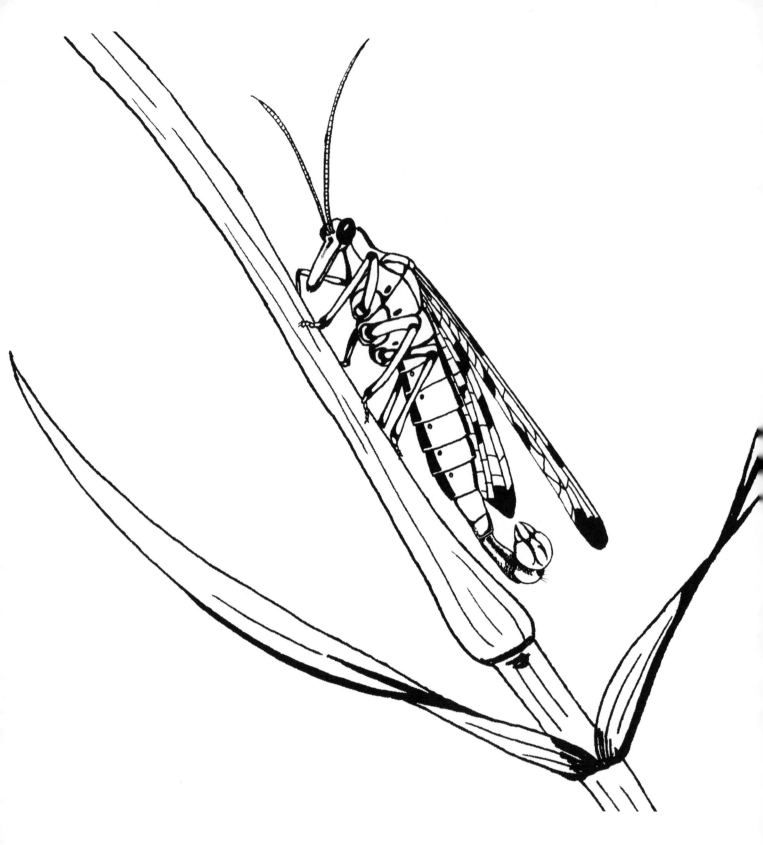

Scorpionflies

These insects are not true flies. They have four wings and a long snout. The name 'scorpionfly' refers to the clasping organ on the end of a male's abdomen that resembles a scorpion's stinger. But don't worry! Scorpionflies are harmless and do not sting or bite. Adult scorpionflies are **scavengers**. Why are scavengers an important part of an ecosystem?

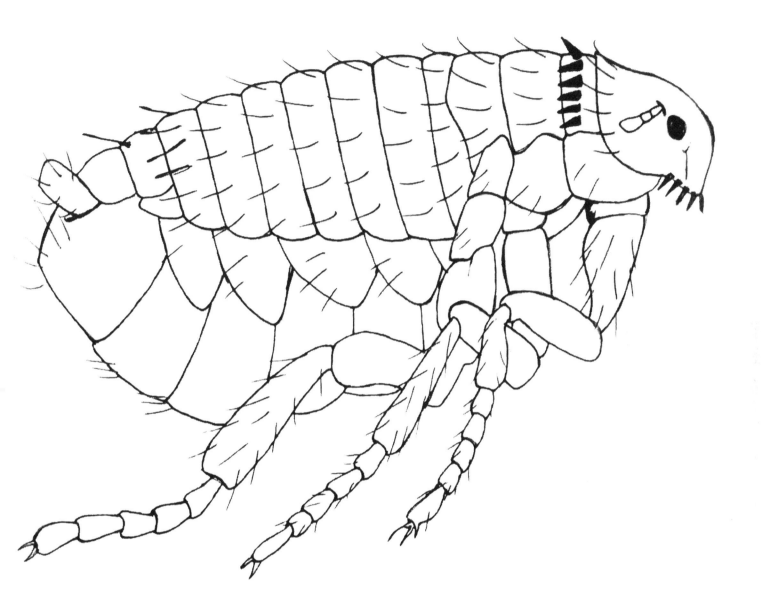

Fleas

Fleas are **ectoparasites** that suck up the blood of their host animal through tiny, needle-like mouthparts called stylets. These wingless insects are so small that we needed to look through a microscope in order to draw this picture. Fleas can jump incredibly high! If you could jump like a flea, you would be able to jump over the Washington Monument in Washington, D.C.

Armoured Ground Cricket

Some crickets don't jump! This large armoured ground cricket slowly crawls over rocky ground in search of food. These insects are **omnivorous**. Sharp spikes and spines on the thorax and legs protect these slow moving crickets from predators.

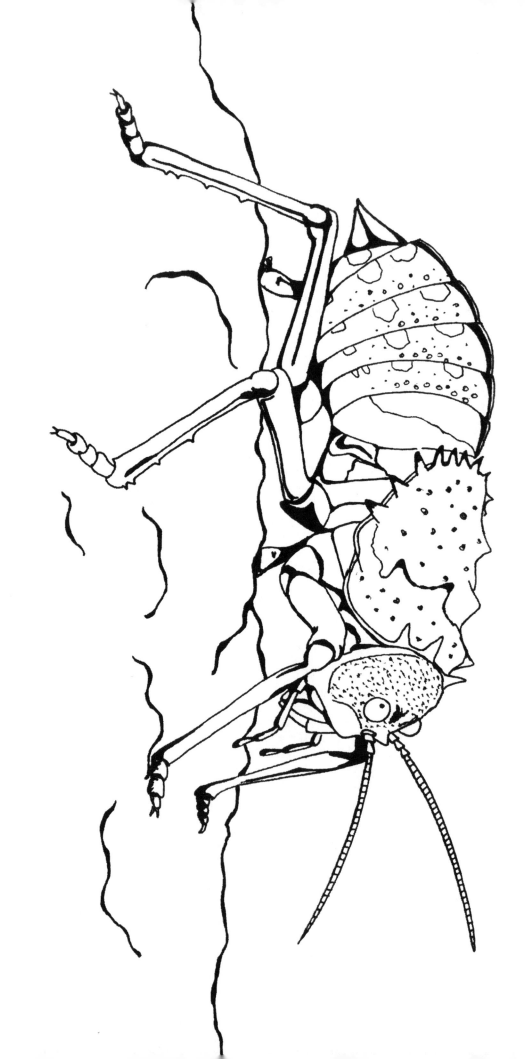

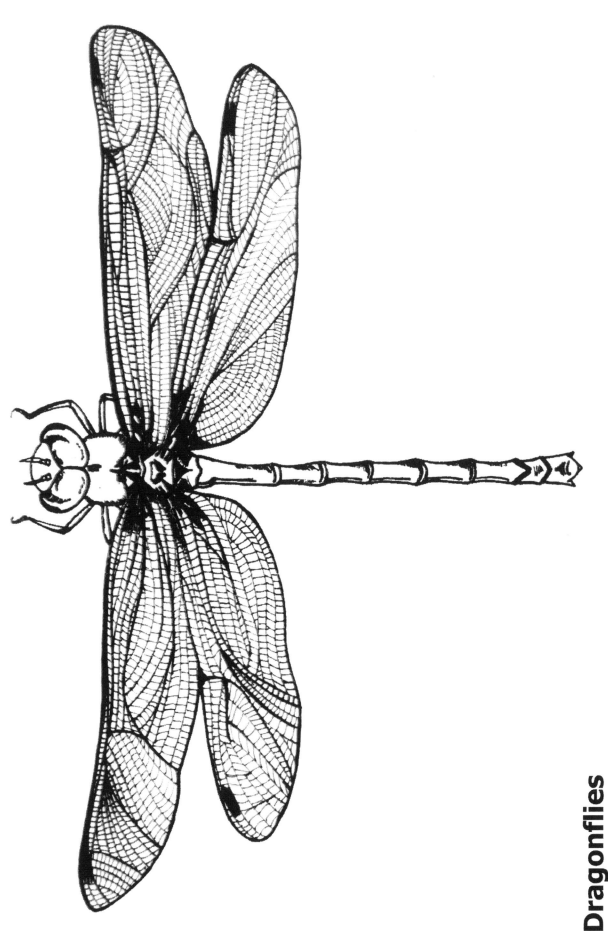

Dragonflies

Dragonflies are some of the best fliers in the insect world! They use their four powerful wings to hover, dart and zoom around ponds and lakes. Adult dragonflies eat mosquitoes. The aquatic larvae, called **naiads,** are important predators in freshwater systems. The eyes of dragonflies wrap almost all the way around their heads, giving them a 300 degree field of vision.

Drawing Exercise

Learn to draw an atlas moth! Use the grid as a guide to help you draw this insect. Draw yours in the blank grid below.

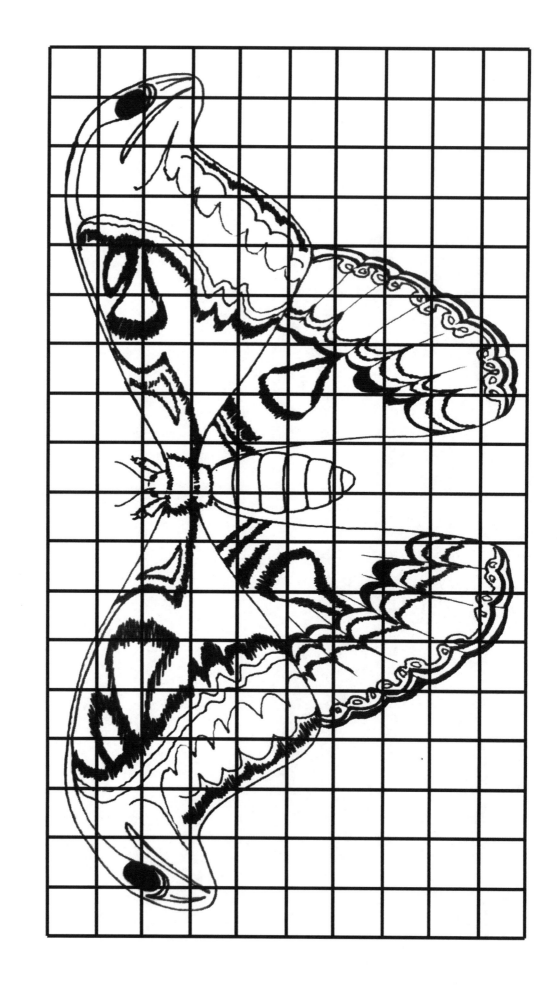

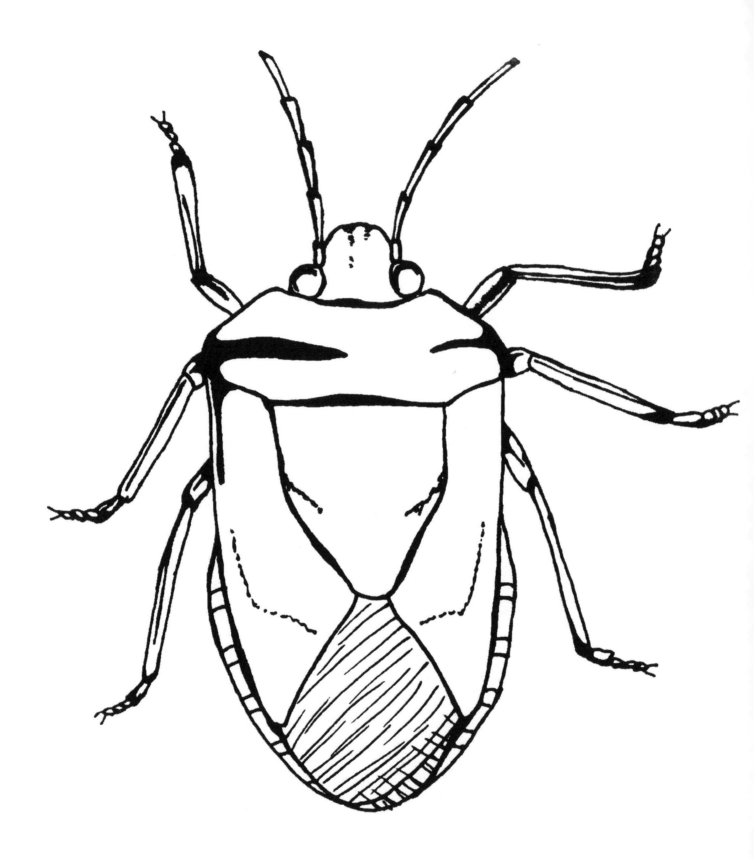

Stink Bug (dorsal)

Stink bugs are true bugs but sometimes people mistake them for beetles! True bugs have wings that are half **sclerotized** and half membranous, and cross over their backs in an X shape. Beetles forewings are fully hardened and meet in a straight line down their backs. This is one way you can tell these insects apart.

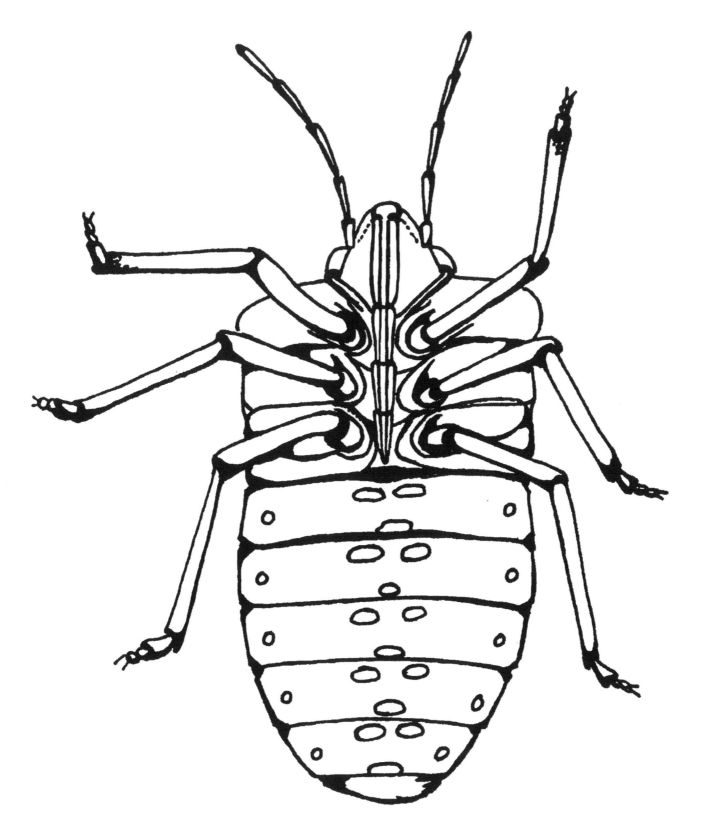

Stink Bug (ventral)

Another way to tell the difference between true bugs and beetles is to look at the mouthparts. True bugs have a rostrum, or piercing-sucking mouthpart. It acts like a giant needle. Beetles always have chewing mouthparts. If you're confused, flip your insect over and look at the mouthparts!

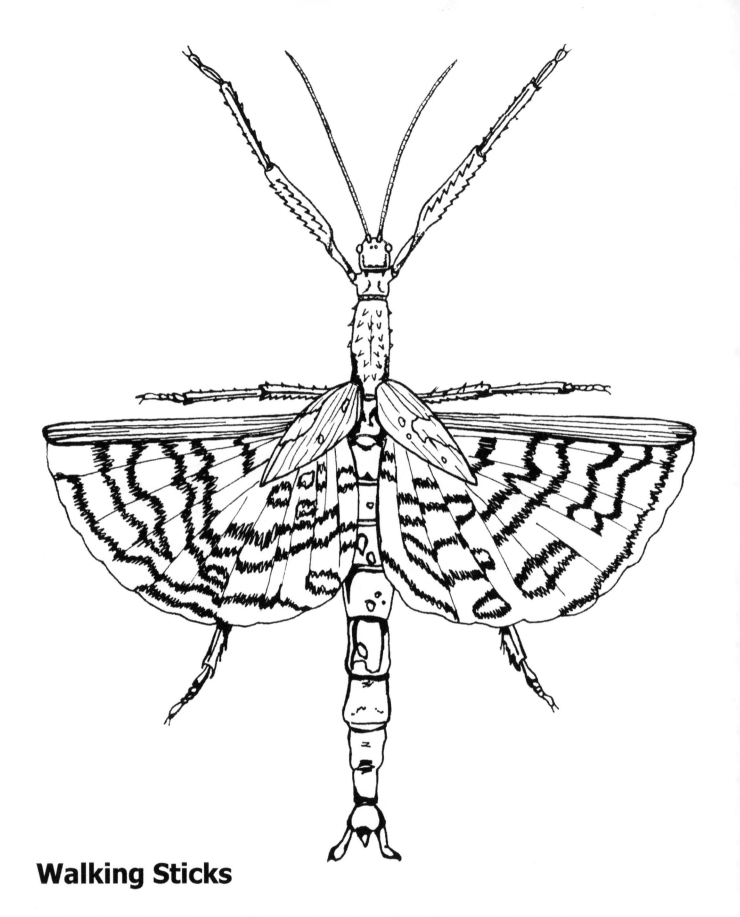

Walking Sticks

This giant walking stick is found in the jungles of Papua New Guinea, a country north of Australia. Stick insects are masters of **crypsis**. This insect looks so much like a stick that it even has tiny thorns all over its body. The hind wings look like dried leaves and the forewings look like they are covered in lichen and moss.

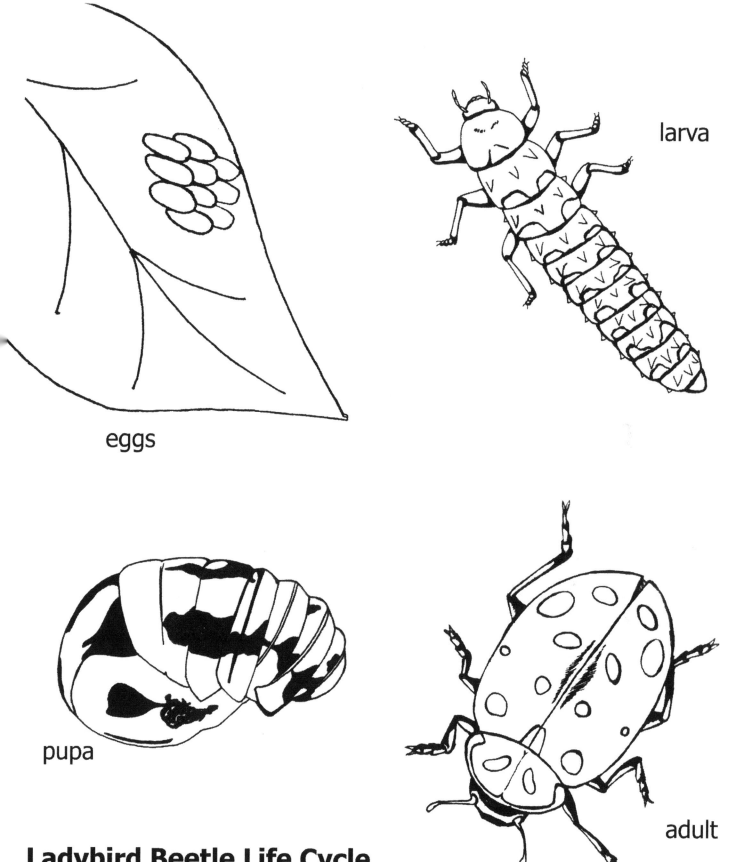

eggs

larva

pupa

adult

Ladybird Beetle Life Cycle

Ladybird beetles, commonly called ladybugs, go through complete **metamorphosis**. Eggs hatch into larvae that pupate into the adult form. The larvae look completely different from the adults! Can you think of other insects that go through complete metamorphosis?

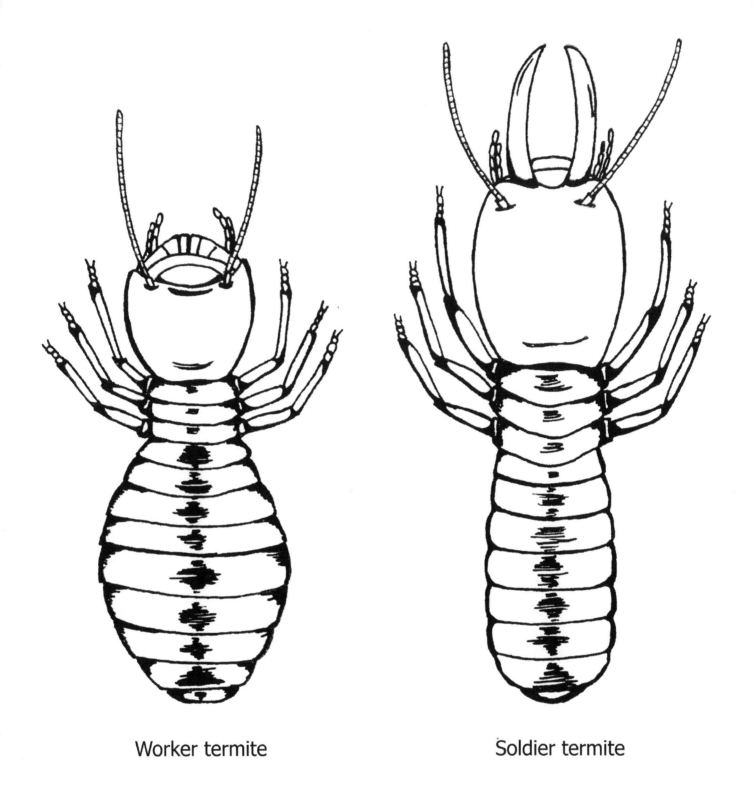

Worker termite   Soldier termite

Termites

Termites are **eusocial** insects that live together in a colony. Workers are usually pale in color. They build the nest, forage for food and take care of the **brood**. Soldier termites usually have large mandibles and work to defend the nest by biting intruders. Queen termites are very large. They lay millions of eggs to keep the colony numbers strong.

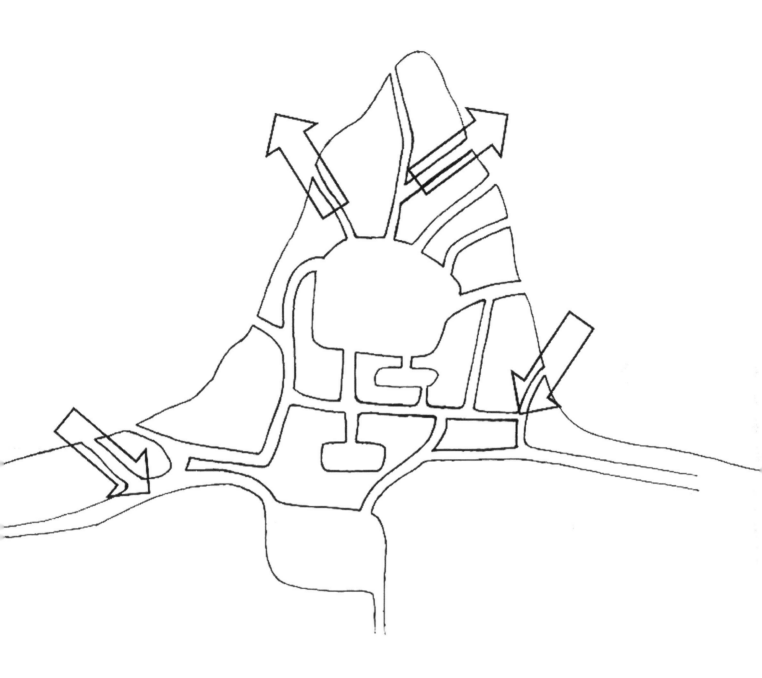

Subterranean Termite Mound

Color the two arrows at the top of the mound red. Color the two arrows pointing into the bottom of the mound blue. Warm air (red arrows) escapes from the top of the termite nest. This creates suction to bring in cool air (blue arrows) near the base of the nest. Subterranean termites are able to regulate the air temperature in their mounds using these tunnels and chimneys!

Praying Mantids

These insects are top predators and use their **raptorial** front legs to capture flying insects. The spines on the inner surfaces of the legs help to keep the prey from escaping. Mantids come in all sizes and colors. Some even look like flower petals and sticks! They are called "praying" mantids because of the way they hold their front legs.

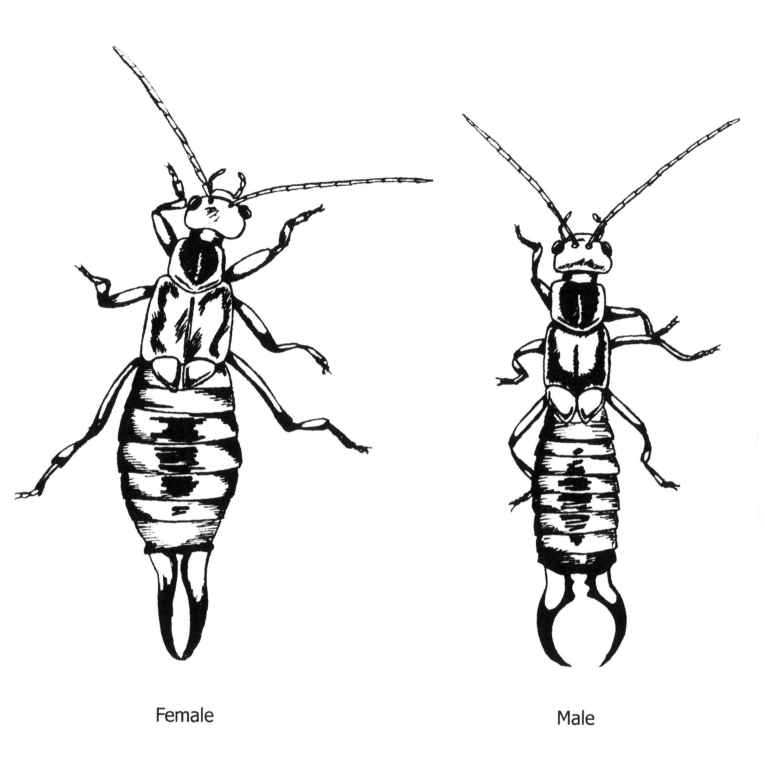

Female

Male

Earwigs

Earwigs are small, flat, brown insects that can run very quickly. The pincers on the end of the abdomen are actually modified **cerci**. Some of the larger species can pinch a bit so handle with care! Females have straight cerci and males have curved cerci. These insects are very misunderstood! They eat pollen, nectar, plants and insects. They do NOT eat ear wax, ears or skin. They do NOT climb into peoples' ears and eat brains.

Silverfish

These shy insects are small, flat and covered in silvery scales. They run very quickly and hide in damp places like basements and bathroom cupboards. They do not bite but they can eat holes in your sweaters and the pages of your books! This is because they are capable of digesting cellulose, a substance found in plant cell walls.

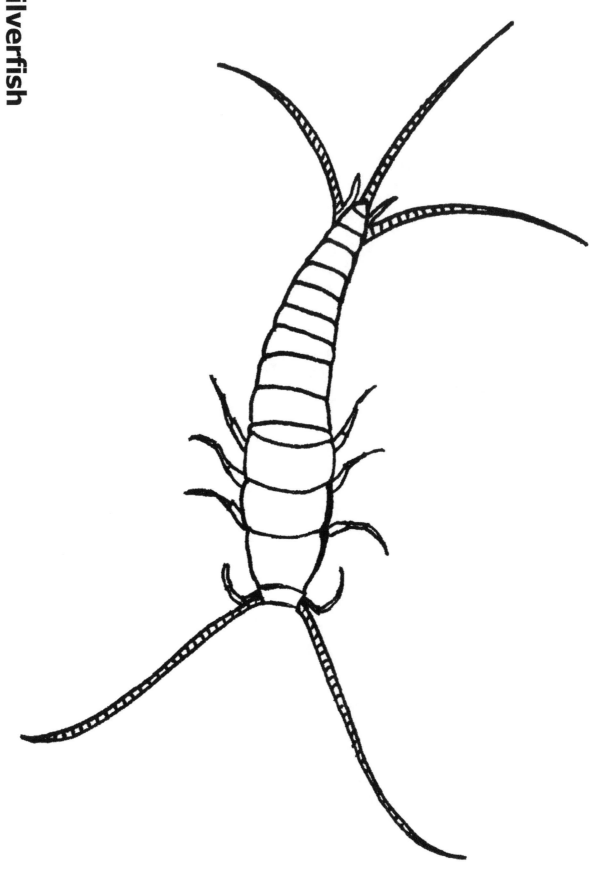

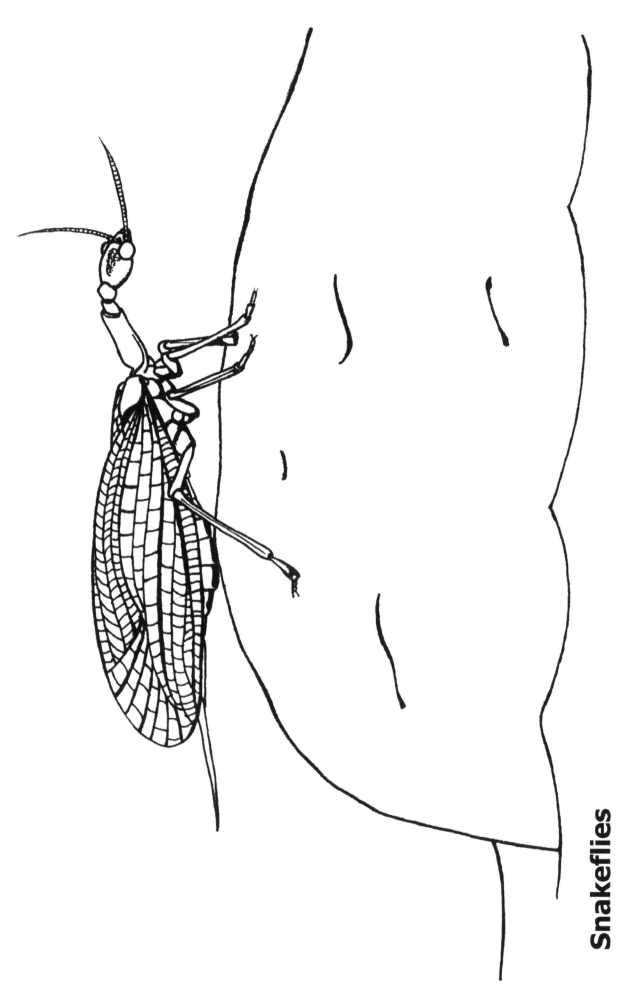

Snakeflies

These insects have four wings and are found in forest habitats. With their long necks and flat heads they resemble snakes! This is why these animals are commonly called snakeflies. No need to fear them though; they have no venom and do not bite or sting. The drawing above shows a female snakefly with a a long **ovipositor** on the end of her abdomen. What does an ovipositor do?

Drawing Exercise

Learn to draw a ground cricket!

Use the grid as a guide to help you draw this insect. Draw yours in the blank grid below.

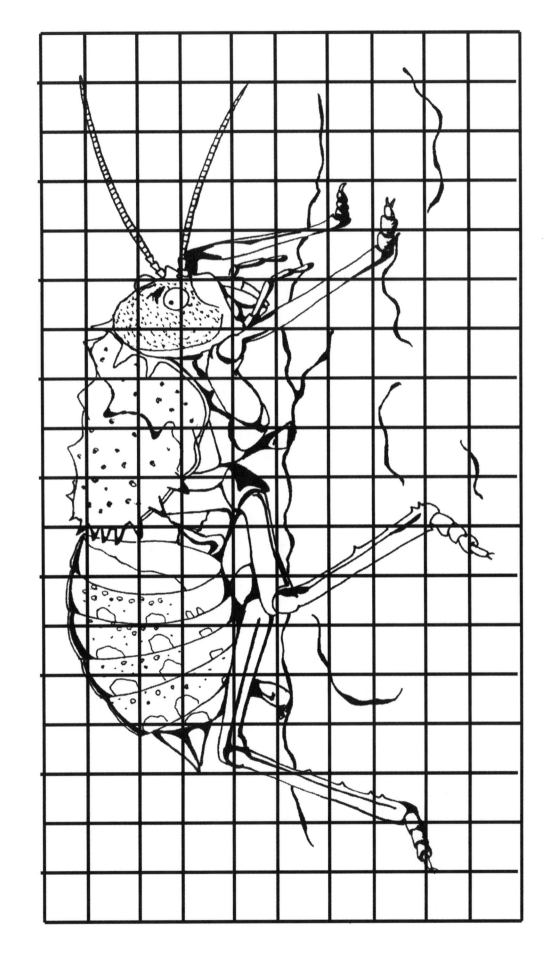

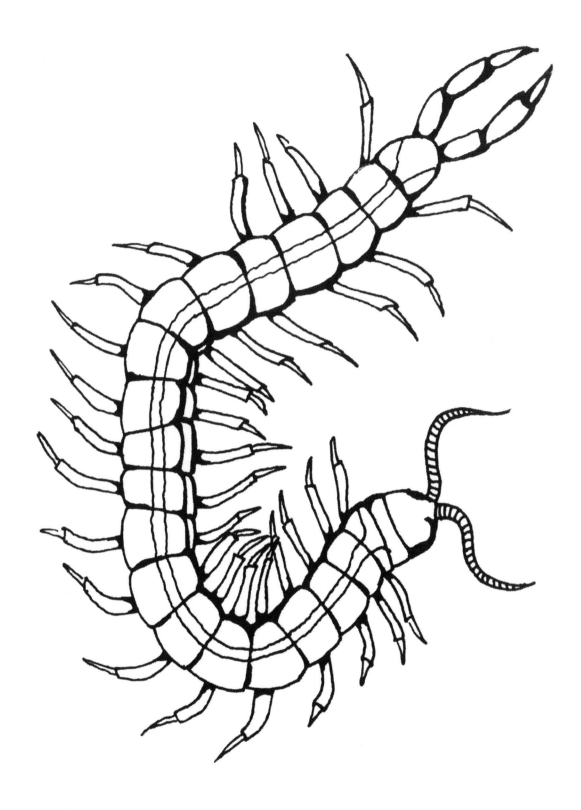

Centipedes

Centipedes are long animals with one pair of legs on each body segment. The first pair of legs is modified into fang-like structures called **forcipules**! They use these to inject venom into their prey. Some venom can be very dangerous to humans so you should not touch a centipede. If you are rolling rocks and see one, it will likely run away very fast and try to hide in a crevice or hole in the soil.

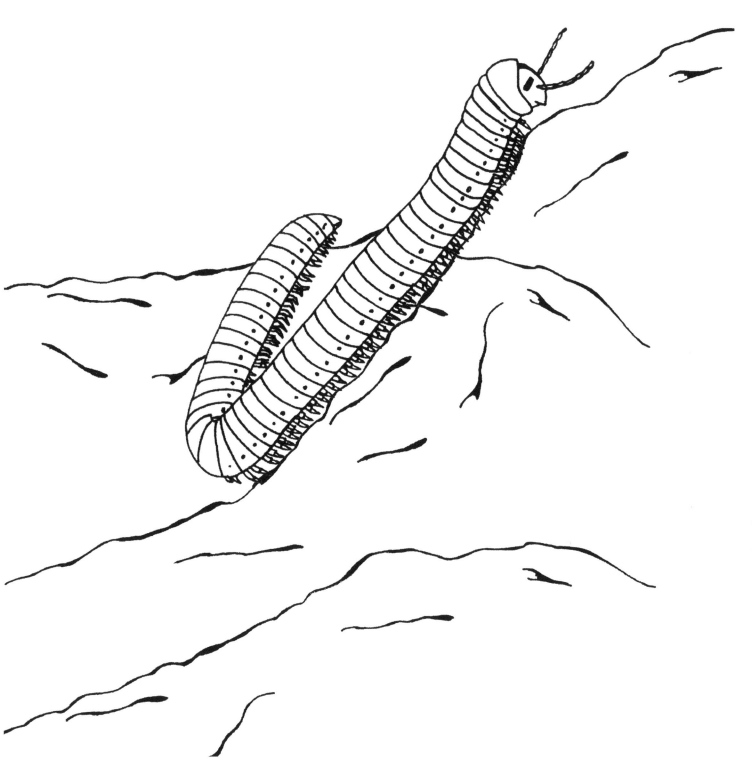

Millipedes

Millipedes look a lot like centipedes, but look closer! These long animals have fused body segments so it actually looks like they have TWO pairs of legs on a single segment! Also, millipedes move slowly and eat rotting plants and **fungi**. When threatened they will curl up and some even leak toxins from special glands near their legs. These toxins taste horrible and act as a deterrent to predators. How many legs does this millipede have?

Tarantulas

Tarantulas are covered in special sensory hairs called setae. These spiders spin silk, but do not catch prey in a web. They are **ambush** hunters! Many people think tarantulas are black or brown, but the spider drawn above is actually blue! As she matures, her legs will turn purple, her head will turn green and her abdomen will be red!

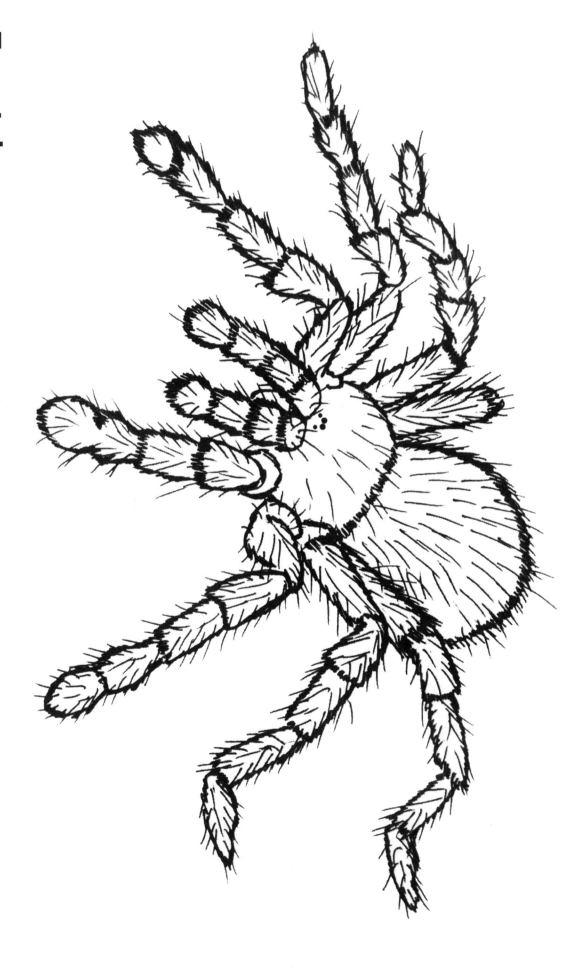

Scorpions

With strong claws and a stinging tail, scorpions are top arthropod predators. These animals are **arachnids.** They have a **cephalothorax,** an abdomen and eight legs. Scorpion venom can be dangerous to humans so it's best to observe these animals and not touch them. If you visit the desert, bring an ultraviolet flashlight with you and you can see these amazing animals "glow" in the dark. This is called fluorescence.

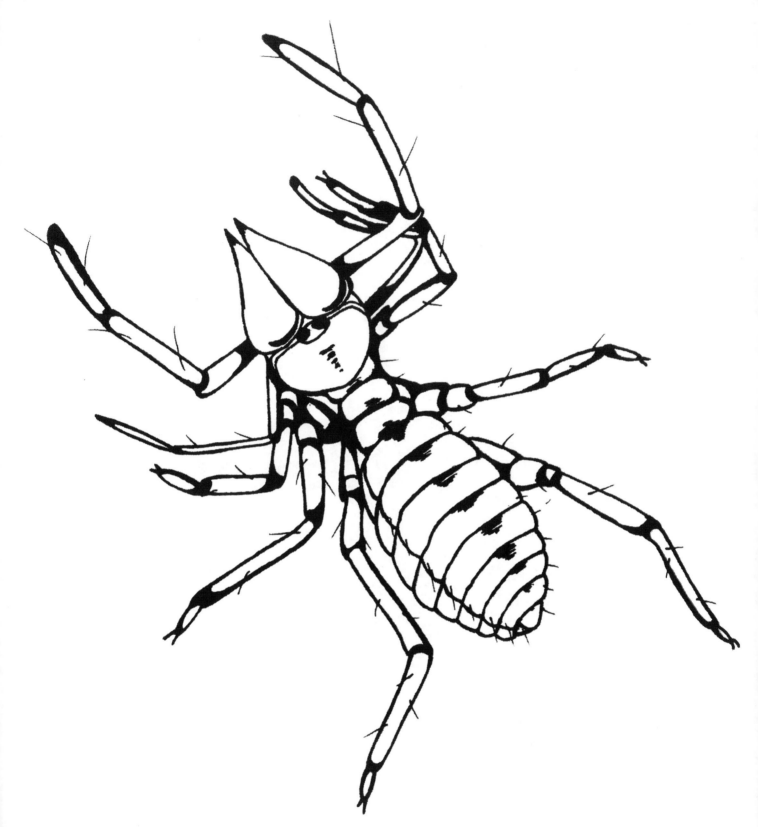

Solifuges

Solifuge arachnids are related to spiders and scorpions. They have eight legs and live in **arid** habitats. These animals go by lots of different common names like sun spiders, camel spiders, and wind scorpions. They have no venom! They use their long leg-like **pedipalps** to grasp prey and their huge **chelicerae** to crush prey during feeding.

GLOSSARY

ambush - to attack by surprise from a concealed location

anterior - located near the front or head

arachnids - arthropods with eight legs, two body sections, chelicerae and pedipalps

arid - dry or desert-like

arthropod - an animal with an exoskeleton, bilateral symmetry (where the right side of the animal is the same as the left side of the animal) and ring-like segments. Insects, arachnids and crustaceans are examples of arthropods.

brood - the offspring or young of animals

cephalothorax - a body section on arachnids made up of the fused head and thorax

cerci - paired segmented appendages on the abdomens of insects that usually function as sensory organs

chelicerae - special mouthparts of arachnids. In spiders they are fang-like. In scorpions and solifuges they are chelate, or claw-like.

crypsis - the ability of an organism to blend into its environment and avoid detection

dimorphism - two different forms of a single species in body shape, color or size

ectoparasites - organisms that live on the outside of their host animal and feed on the host or at
the expense of the host

eusocial - an insect society with defined tasks for individuals, cooperative care of young and multiple generations living together

forcipules - the first pair of legs on a centipede that are modified into venom claws

fungi - a group of organisms made up of yeasts, molds and mushrooms

gregarious - living in a loose group

labellum- a sponging mouthpart on house flies

metamorphosis - 'meta' means change and 'morph' means body; a change in body form

mimicry - when an animal acts or looks like a different object or animal

naiad - the aquatic, immature stage of a dragonfly, mayfly, or stonefly

GLOSSARY

omnivorous - eating both plants and animals

ovipositor - the egg-laying organ on a female insect

pedipalps - special mouthparts of arachnids that help to bring food to the chelicerae. In scorpions, they are claws. In spiders and solifuges they are leg-like.

pronotum - the upper part of the first segment on the thorax; often shield-like.

raptorial - adapted for grasping or seizing prey

saltatorial - adapted for jumping or leaping

scavenger - an animal that feeds on dead or dying animals or plant matter

sclerotized - hardened or thickened

subterranean – underneath the surface of the ground

tarsal pads - fleshy pads on the bottom of an insect's feet

58214895R00021

Made in the USA
Lexington, KY
05 December 2016